THINK LIKE A BARTENDER

THINK
LIKE A
BARTENDER

RECIPES FOR LIFE

L.D. MORROW

ISBN: 978-0-578-44889-3

If found, please return to:

_____

_____

_____

_____

DEDICATION

To every toast, cheer, laugh, tear, shot, hangover,
hangunder I ever experienced
at a bar. To those liquid therapists who
listened and loved while they poured
and pondered.

INGREDIENTS

ACKNOWLEDGMENTS

To my friends who encouraged me,
My family that sustained me,
And the following bar and restaurants
that helped influence this book:

Agave- NYC

Settepani-NYC

Red Rooster-NYC

West 3rd Common- NYC

Sexy Taco -NYC

Mama Sushi-NYC

Lido - NYC

67 Orange-NYC

Harlem Food Bar -NYC

Angel of Harlem- NYC

Mamajuana -NYC

W XYZ Bar -NYC

The Cecil - NYC

Barawine-NYC

La Diagonal- NYC

Bond St.-NYC

Row House -NYC

Raines Law Room-NYC

The Row Harlem-NYC

Apotheke- NYC

Rocco's WeHo-LA

Skybar- Mandarin/Las Vegas

PUMP-LA

Charthouse- NJ

The Abbey-LA

Sawyer-LA

Brotherhood of Thieves- MA

The Roosevelt Bar- NO

The Palace- MIA

Caliente Cab -NYC

PRE-DRINKS

While working on my undergraduate degree, my communications professor gave one particularly interesting assignment that semester...we were told to secure a part-time job in the service industry. The suggestion was either as a host or server at a restaurant. While most of us thought our professor was crazy to assign such a silly and seemingly easy task for an entire semester's grade, I was surprised to learn a lifelong lesson.

For me, the goal was to find a restaurant that was close to my apartment and where I liked the food. #poorcollegestudent. I was finally hired at a casual Irish restaurant. After going through training, which included shadowing the waitstaff, host station and bartender, I felt ready to make an easy

A in the class. Shheeeiiiiittttt (please re-read that word as it was written). This assignment was TO DATE one of the hardest jobs I've ever had!

Initially, I was frustrated at all of the customers' requests, complaints and what seemed to be a never ending barrage of insatiability. "My food is too hot. My fries are cold. Can I have your number? This drink is too weak/too strong. Can I use your discount? Can I get an extra this or that?

Slowly, after a few broken plates, promises and harsh complaints, I became very good at remembering orders and listening to what customers were either saying or trying to say. Then it happened. One day, the regular bartender called out sick. Twenty minutes later, the manager was told the backup bartender also could not make it in either. With the after work crowd minutes away from rushing the door, the manager had a decision to make. Since I was the newest employee and he knew this was for a class, I was selected to be the "fill in bartender" for the night. After a 30-minute crash course on 10 basic cocktails, how to pour, dress, prep and clean, I was thrown to the wolves! Rum and coke, vodka and cranberry, a basic margarita ... not a problem. If an old fashioned or a dirty martini was ordered, I smiled with confidence, placed a napkin down in front of the customer and ran to the back to find the ingredients. By the end of the shift I was completely wiped, but fascinated with the joy I experienced serving and getting to know these initial strangers.

In the months that followed, I continued to be drawn to the bartender's role. I was not a "drinker" at the time, but became mesmerized with the various combinations of spirits and recipes that needed to be mastered to have a successful bar and happy customers.

The ability to listen, recall and make one amazing cocktail after another was intriguing to me. From that moment on, I have had a 'healthy' fascination with bars, bartenders and drinks. Since you are wondering, not only did I receive an A in my communications class, but I went on to attend and finish a local bartending course and worked at a few bars for several years afterwards.

Am I still a Bartender?…Nope. Soooooo, why would I write a book called, Think Like a Bartender- Recipes for Life?? The nerve, right?!

Well, although I no longer bartend, the lessons I learned behind the bar have stayed with me through my entire corporate career. Every job I've had since then… I've been making cocktails…. sales cocktails, marketing mixtures, contractual summaries on the rocks, etc. you get it. In addition to that, I have met some of my best friends at bars and I've started (and ended) relationships at a bar. I conceived and created my first non-profit business at a bar. I've lost friends and shed tears… all at a bar. And it was not just the physical location or the drink specials that caused these things to happen…it was also the skill and interaction with amazing bartenders.

Bartenders are the eyes and ears of the establishment and are the ones ultimately responsible for providing a good time, monitoring customer behavior, collecting payment for services rendered and being a friend, counselor, bouncer and teacher all at the same time.

This book will share many of the amazing lessons I learned or re-learned while making and enjoying cocktails. This book can be consumed by everyone (over 21). Even if you have never had a drink...I bet you know someone who has, so you will be able to relate to many of the examples in the book! Each chapter not only includes a relevant comical illustration, but also has one of my favorite cocktail recipes with a fun twist on the title. The goal of this book is not to advocate or encourage excessive drinking, but to simply draw some interesting, creative parallels in lessons we need to remember...lessons I learned while making and having a cocktail or three! So grab a seat at my bar and let's get started!

CHEERS!

DRUNK HISTORY

On September 30, 1982, NBC premiered a new show called Cheers. During its 11 year tenure, Cheers was one of the most popular shows of all time and received multiple awards, including 13 Emmy Award nominations for its first season alone. The storyline was simple. Assemble a cast of regulars at a fictitious bar in Boston who share their day-to-day experiences and lives with each other all while drinking and/or working.

Now, I was just a kid when the show first aired and I didn't know much about bars or drinking. But one thing I could quickly understand...everyone wants to go to a place where they feel comfortable, recognized, well liked or at least a place to meet friends. One of the famous lines from the theme song of the show was "Sometimes you want to go, where everybody knows your name."

If you frequent bars or lounges, think about one or two of your favorite bartenders. Do you have a local watering hole or favorite spot in the neighborhood you like to go to? Visualize the moment you walk in and the bartender sees you. Are you the type that always drinks the same thing so they are already preparing the usual? Do you enjoy having some light conversation with them and hearing about the specials or whatever innovative creation is on the menu for that evening? Regardless of the answer, you know there's more to preparing your drink than a clean glass, ice and your favorite spirit.

From the bartender's perspective, if you are memorable, have a great attitude and display positive energy, you may find yourself as a favorite customer. The type that before you come in and sit down, your drink is already being placed in front of you.

And it's always been that way! The history of bartending dates back to ancient times and even then pubs were used as a place for social gatherings. And for hundreds of years, the bartender has played an important role in the creation and enjoyment of delicious libations for thirsty patrons. And even from the moment of the first bartender, Jeremiah "Jerry" P. Thomas, there were expectations of quality and service. This is one of the oldest professions (no, not that one) steeped in history and presented with pride.

Speaking of history, do you know where the word alcohol originated from? The earliest traces come from the Arabic term' al kuhl', which means the finer thing or the essence of. The word was specifically used to describe antimony, a mineral Arabs made into a fine black powder Arab women used as eye make-up. By the early 17th century, antimony begins to refer to anything made from or taken from an essence, particularly distillation. For example, al kuhl of wine meant the essence of wine. Later it simply became 'alcohol'. This means delicious cocktails and adult beverages today carry a name used by women in Egypt for eyeshadow. Kinda gives a whole new meaning to the term "shade".

Whether you drink wine and spirits or water and sprite, you have to give credit to the overall resiliency of this industry, also known as Big Alcohol. The production of alcohol can be traced back as far as 12,000 years! Some countries had, and still have, laws that regulate the sale and consumption of alcoholic beverages. Some countries even ban such activities entirely. But don't fret, alcohol will still be around for hundreds of years to come and so will those who appreciate it!

PROHIBITION

WHAT CHA NEED

2 oz. Bourbon
½ oz. sweet vermouth
1 dash of bitters
1 cup of ice cubes
1 maraschino cherry for garnish

WHAT CHA DO

Add ice in a mixing glass. Add vermouth, then bourbon, and stir. Strain into a cocktail glass. Dash it with the bitters and add cherry.

WHAT ARE YOU SERVING?

If you have ever tried your luck on a dating site like Tinder, Match or EHarmony, you know how important it is to keep your religion. Now hold on....not the church religion you may be thinking. On a majority of these dating sites it's critical to be able to separate the real from the fake.......in order to do that, you must regularly attend Bye-Bull Study. Bye-Bull study will help in the ability to figure out fact from bullshit. This is also a necessary step to get to know the 'real' person.

Let's face it, we all are guilty of misrepresenting a fact or two from time to time. We do it to create a more attractive 'menu' of ourselves and a more appealing image to draw in the right customers.

With over 20 years of corporate experience, there have been several times I've interviewed prospective candidates for vacant positions on my team. After a while, you become somewhat of an expert when it comes to separating fact from fiction on resumes. While it is expected for a person to try to present their best selves on paper, it can be dangerous if examples or supporting documentation are lacking in regards to a specific claim about experience.

Many moons ago, I was interviewing candidates to fill a vacant position on my team. The job description was very clear on the technical skill set required for consideration. After combing over several resumes suggested from human resources, there were three candidates I was ready to start phone interviewing. One particular candidate had a stellar resume that reflected multiple years of experience in CRM platforms as well as an expert proficiency level in Excel. Excited, I could not wait to hear of a few real-world, on-the-job examples this candidate could use to support their claim.

The first 15 minutes of the phone interview went great. The person was an excellent communicator, appeared to be a great listener and spoke very highly of their former companies. This led me to believe this candidate had a high level of emotional intelligence and could fit very well with my current team and company. Finally, we got down to skill sets. One interview question was, "Give me an example of a time you used Salesforce and Excel to achieve a particular business objective." The candidate danced around their ability to be a strong verbal communicator and how spreadsheets were very important when communicating with the client. They then went on to say that you are only as strong as your 'sales force' and the team should all work together for a common goal. Blink.........Blink.

Although there is such a thing as a sales force, a group of employees who sell one or more items, I was specifically talking about the application Salesforce. Clearly, the candidate overrepresented what they could provide. Disappointed that this was the true version of the candidate, I no longer considered the person for the role. The "menu offerings" did not match what is available.

So what is a menu? A menu is typically a list of available items for selection and/or purchase at a restaurant, bar or other establishment that offers a service. Menus provide very important information to customers such as detailed descriptions of what you will be receiving. Whether in print or digital, we are all accustomed to selecting items we desire from a list of available choices. When ordering at a restaurant for dine-in or delivery, an overall successful experience is usually contingent on whether or not the items listed are available and will be presented as described. I'm sure we can all relate to a time we were scanning a food menu and a picture of something delicious caught our eye. After reading the description, the mental decision is made to select the most desired choice....... only to be met with the disappointing news that the particular item is no longer available or simply out of stock! It's a deflating, frustrating feeling that forces you to make an alternative choice or simply leave and go to another establishment.

Are you aware of your 'personal' menu? When people take a look at what you say you are offering in a job or relationship, are they met with satisfaction or disappointment?

For example, when you look at my personal menu what you will not see in the visual offerings are tight dresses, heavy makeup and high heels. Not only is that not on my menu...but you actually might want to visit a different restaurant...on the other side of town!

Knowing WHO you are, WHAT you truly have to offer and HOW you are perceived is an extremely important piece of knowledge when presenting yourself to others. These are also key components to 'how' you will be remembered. Have you ever checked your phone contacts after a night out at a bar or business networking event? Sometimes you may have to place reminders in the notes section of your phone to jog your memory about a particular person. These new and interesting people you met who were clearly impactful enough that you added them in your phone but you create some catchy reminder to jolt your memory the next day. When I think of some of the names I have given people in my phone just to remember who they are until I determine if they are worth a permanent, valued position are hilarious. But sometimes they can backfire. To this day, I still don't know who Ken-Pimple-Cookie, Crystal $20 and Sean Whiskey and Wings are.

Knowledge and truth in advertising of your 'personal offerings' is just as important as a bartender being aware of the inventory for various reds, whites and different brands of vodka available. I remember pissing plenty of customers off when I said, "Uhhhh, I'm not sure, let me go ask. I was supposed to be the knowledgeable one and should have had the correct info.

The same can be said in terms of drink preparation. If a bartender does not know how to make a cocktail you requested, you begin to question the experience and skill set of that person. Unfortunately, this distrust can seep into expectations of not only the wait staff, but also the food that is served... even the establishment. Great bartenders take pride in not only their skill set, but also their knowledge of the menu. And if a particular drink or brand is not available, they are ready to offer a comparable or alternate suggestion.

So.....what are you serving? Are you stretching the ingredients and descriptions on your resume... lying about your education when the only certificates of achievement you have or will have are a birth certificate and a death certificate? Are you advertising love and compassion for an interested party, only for them to be met with lust and condescending attitudes? Remember this: If you find yourself attracting unsolicited customers to your personal 'life bar', take a look at what you are advertising. It might be time for a menu update!

ALWAYS KNOW WHAT YOU TRULY HAVE TO
OFFER AND KEEP IT REAL!

POUR FAVOR

WHAT CHA NEED

1.5 oz. Premium Vodka
1 oz. olive brine
1 or 2 olives

WHAT CHA DO

Combine ice, vodka and olive brine
in cocktail shaker. Shake that shyt.
Pour straight up in a chilled martini glass.
Add olive of choice as garnish.

3 STOP LOSING "WAIT"

Growing up, I was your typical nerd. I made straight A's, read every billboard, street sign and book cover out loud and could recite the 23 helping verbs in under 4 seconds (I still can… try me). One of the most exciting times for me was Standardized testing season! The woody smell of a full pencil sharpener, the fear in the eyes of the unprepared and those unfilled circles from a scantron would just give me 9 year old tingles (too much?).

Thursday, March 8, 1984 started out like any other morning for me. My grandmother 'gently' woke me up by turning on loud gospel music and three bright 100 watt light bulbs that beamed down from the ceiling. I brushed my teeth, washed my face and prayed she had not laid out an outfit that consisted of showing my legs or shoulders. This was the morning of another important test! I ran to the kitchen, scarfed down my bowl of Fruit Loops, grabbed my 20-lb backpack and bolted to the car where my grandfather was waiting to take me to school.

Right before I headed out, Nunna (my grandmother) grabbed my arm and said, "Aren't you forgetting something?" I thought to myself, "Pencils...erasers...backup pencils...Nope, I have everything!" She reminded me, "You didn't go kiss your Mom goodbye and show her what you are wearing."

My mother and I had been living with my grandparents since I came home from the hospital as a newborn. Since my grandmother ran her own daycare, she would wake me up and help me get dressed for school while my mom slept in from her night shift as a nurse. The agreement my mom and I had was that no matter what, I would go kiss her goodbye and show her what I was wearing each day. This particular morning, I just did not have time. My goal was to get to school, sharpen my pencils and review for this test!! I told my grandma as I walked out the door, "I don't have time. I have to go! I will kiss her when I get home."

Unfortunately, that never happened. About two hours after I got to school and started taking my tests, I was called to the front office by the principal. One of the parents from my grandmother's daycare came to take me home. My mom had passed away in her sleep. The rest of that day, I sat on her bed, holding my unfinished answer grid, crying and angry. That's the image that remains in my mind to this day when I think about her.

For decades, I carried the weight of guilt for being so busy (at 9 years old) that I missed the last chance to smile, kiss or say goodbye to my mother. Since that day, I have embraced patience and have tried not to be "too thin" with it.

Most of us have gone through stages where we wanted to be healthier and lose a few pounds. This does not only have to be a physical goal, but can be an emotional goal, as well. Losing excess mental baggage can absolutely have its benefits. However, as it relates to patience, losing "wait" can be a bad thing. Patience is something many struggle with maintaining and regulating. Be it career progression, relationships or fitness goals, if we could only control the clock, results would definitely not take as long. When you grow up with grandparents like I did, they walk slower, chew slower and talk slower. I eventually learned not to rush the process and embrace the pace.

As I got older, unfortunately I started having issues with patience. In college, I can remember being so impatient with my love life or lack of it. It was odd to me. I was able to successfully control all other aspects of my life except matters of the heart. I remember one day, my grandfather, JD, was sitting and listening intently to me whine on and on about not finding love. When I stopped to take a breath (and a sip of Jameson), he asked me a question. "What if I said you had to wait five years to meet someone, but when you met them, you would be with them forever? Would you wait?" I replied, "Of course!" Then he said, "But what if I told you that you had to wait ten years to meet your eternal love? Would you wait?" Again I said, "Sure...but...!" He quickly interrupted me. "Why not think about it that way... you could be in the season of patience and the time for you will come." Update: He was right!! A wise man indeed!

When it comes to managing your time with others, in order to be successful, you must work to manage your patience and expectations. In that same vein, when multiple people depend on you at the same time, it can be challenging to always give your best in a timely fashion. Your parents, workplace, significant other, siblings...it's a constant struggle to manage your time.

Are you mentally overweight? Are the heavy life expectations of others starting to put a strain on your emotional joints? You may sometimes feel mentally lethargic... tired and not living up to your best self?

Bartenders can relate because they have a very interesting job. Everyone wants their attention.

Customers have orders, requests and questions. All of them have money and think they should have individual attention and be next in line.

Here's a thought: Have you ever stood in a position of service at the 'bar' of your life? Do you have multiple people waiting for you to tend to their needs? Some of the best bartenders in the business encounter this on a daily basis. Their advice: Take a mental picture of your landscape of customers. Based on the time of approach, remember who's next. Keep your pace. Otherwise this could affect the quality of your 'drink' or the service you are rendering. I've learned that if people are at your bar and they want to be served or desire service, they should understand that you are worth the wait and trying to give the best experience possible. Don't find yourself losing too much 'wait' and end up being emotionally malnourished!

REMEMBER, TAKE YOUR TIME.
YOU ARE WORTH IT!!

SLENDER BENDER

WHAT CHA NEED

1 ½ oz. Premium Blanco Tequila
2 oz. Fresh Lime Juice
¼ oz. Agave
Optional: Cointreau

WHAT CHA DO

Combine all ingredients in a shaker
with ice. Shake until the lactic acid
builds up in your arm.
Pour contents into a glass with ice
(salt rim optional). Use lime to garnish.
Add floater of Cointreau.

YOU'RE FIRED!

A few years ago, after visiting my primary care physician for a routine physical and blood work, it was revealed that I suffered from a condition called AVD. After the diagnosis, I began to research others who suffered from this condition. I eventually found a great support group for AVD sufferers and survivors.

AVD, also known as Anal Vision Distortion, occurs when you have a hard time 'seeing' your 'ass' in situations that may not be good for you or doing things for people that are undeserving of your time.

When I think back, if I ever had a blemish or dark blip on my career map it would be the one time I decided to pursue a role more based on title and compensation than the overall experience including corporate culture and work/ life balance. I interviewed for a top Fortune 50 consumer products company unaware of how it would ultimately cause me, for the first time, to fire myself!

The recruiting process for this role was unlike any I had encountered. Once I received an offer for the position, only then, was I introduced to the person who would be my manager. After a couple of weeks of on-boarding, my supervisor asked me a question about my salary and bonus levels. Clearly feeling like I could trust this person professionally (after all, this was my boss), I shared the information. Little did I know, my salary was very close to my managers.

I regretted sharing this information because immediately after that and for several months that followed, my boss became unnecessarily irate, frustrated and critical of any and EVERYTHING I did. Memos were sent to superiors stating the concern that I lacked the necessary communication skills for the role and wasn't a team player. It seemed like anything I did was met with critique and negative feedback. I even went so far as to have a colleague who had been with the company for 20 years complete a simple project for me. My manager's feedback was that it was sub par and far below company expectations. Even though I had a seasoned colleague complete the project to prove the point that I wasn't getting fair treatment. I got so frustrated and depressed that I cried before going to work, cried after I got home, questioned my ability as a leader and a significant contributor and even started taking anti-anxiety meds. Even my attempts to interact with HR did not help. It was at that moment I decided I needed to fire myself...I Quit!

Continuing in this environment with the lack of support and an increased amount of doubt, would not only affect my ability to do my job, but would ultimately seep into the core of who I was. So I walked away..... without knowing what job I was going to get next, but the value of regaining my sanity was priceless. In the end, it was one of the best career decisions of my life.

Not only is it necessary to fire yourself from negative situations, sometimes you also have to fire yourself from negative people that don't encourage growth or help contribute to you being your best self! I have friends and relatives to this day that I still love but are not an active part of my life due to their unhealthy energy.

A lack of challenge can have the same effect as a negative environment. Even though feeling settled or content in your career has its pros. Remember, great things never came from comfort zones. One plus to doing the same thing over and over is that you find it takes less effort to complete tasks... usually because you have done it so many times.

However, a major con to a lack of being challenged is that it can cause brain atrophy. John F. Kennedy once said, "There are risks and costs to action. But they are far less than the long range risks of comfortable inaction."

You also tend to make more mistakes when you are too comfortable. You become less aware of your surroundings and can get lulled into a comatose state. I've always felt that one great goal in life is to continue to challenge yourself, hone your particular craft and never stop learning! A satisfying career should mean you are able to constantly show your worth and are adequately compensated and appreciated for it. My first bar manager told me, "Each day you leave work, you are already paid for that day. It's your job to show your value each and every new day."

I'm sure we all know or had a favorite bartender who suddenly up and left their job...sometimes without another gig secured. Many of the bartenders interviewed for this book feel one of the smartest things they have done in their professional lives is realize when it's time to move on. Maybe they have been working at the bar for so long only the same people come in. It could also be they are no longer challenged with the cocktail orders or have a horrible relationship with the staff or management. Whatever the reason, they realized that the cost of staying far outweighed the cost of leaving.

When is the last time you fired yourself? Some-times we get to the point where things that were once important to us, are no longer desired. I have actually fired myself not only from a job, but also from friendships and relationships. Get com-fortable terminating circumstances in your life. At a certain stage in life we have completed a lot of things on our 'bucket list', but as you mature, your 'Fuck It" list starts to have more depth because of things you no longer find necessary. Pleasing everyone...Fuck It! Holding your tongue...Fuck It!! Staying in a job you hate...Fuc........wait, wait, wait. Now don't go quitting without having a plan and trying to sue me! But...fuck it!

By constantly re-evaluating what's important in life, you will find yourself leaving many different types of 'jobs'. Remember, it's always best to choose to leave before you are asked to! Regardless if it's in life or love, always take care of the things that are important to you. Take care of yourself and mind your P's and Q's!

Side note: Did you know that phrase has roots in alcohol? Back in England, drinks were served in pints and quarts. If a fight broke out, the bartender would yell to mind your pints and quarts. Over time it became P's and Q's! Crazy right?!

KNOWING WHEN TO LEAVE IS JUST AS
IMPORTANT AS LEAVING!

LEAVE SMILING

WHAT CHA NEED

1 ½ oz. Premium Gin (I prefer Hendricks)
¾ oz. fresh lemon juice
¾ oz. simple syrup
3 cucumber slices, 2 more for garnish
3 fresh basil 'leaves'

WHAT CHA DO

Muddle cucumber, basil and syrup
in a cocktail shaker.
Add ice, lemon juice and gin.
Shake well and strain into a
rocks glass with ice.
Garnish with 2 cucumbers

5 HOW TO MASTER 'BAIT'

A soft stroke, a gentle pull, that perfectly timed moment that can make you come again and again. We've all been there. Think about it...you say you are going to stop in a bar or restaurant for one...two drinks at the most and you end up singing Whitney Houston or Journey at a Karaoke bar at 2am.

That's how it starts...You decide to meet a few friends for some great $6 happy hour drinks and $8 appetizers only to end the night with a $400 tab full of wings, fries, shots and $12 cocktails. I'm damn sure guilty of that. It's not that you are weak minded or a pushover...it's just that...you have been successfully masterbaited on! (Passes you a towel to wipe)

After years of working in the service industry, a majority of my professional career has been in sales and customer marketing roles. In all that time, I have come to find that bartenders are, in fact, some of the best sales people I know. It's where I perfected verbal and non-verbal communication and learned the art of the upsell. So how do they do it? I've narrowed it down to three major things I feel bartenders do to keep you re-ordering, happy and tipsy.

THE DEVIL'S IN THE DETAILS.

We know any good bartender can make a drink, but it takes a special type of bartender to remember the little things. As a customer, I'm always impressed not only when a bartender remembers my favorite drink, but also that I was studying for a real estate exam last week or I was out of town for a business trip. Building rapport with your customers and establishing a history will not only create a loyal future interaction, but also move that establishment or bartender to the top of your list when you're in the mood to have a drink.

The same can be said in our daily lives. Think about your current or last relationship. To know that someone was truly listening to you and remembered an important moment or concern you had, not only made you feel good but goes a long way. And as the old adage goes, that's why you have TWO ears and ONE mouth... to listen twice as much as you speak.

ARMED WITH CHARM

It is very understandable that at times bartenders are slammed and too busy to truly give individualized attention. However, acknowledging a customer's presence, smiling and adding their own personal touch to a conversation can lure an unsuspecting patron into multiple future rounds. Depending on the topic, 9 times out of 10, a customer will take a bartender's advice...because of their charm and emotional intelligence.

This does not mean they have a license to lie and make up stories to make it seem like there is more in common. But when a bartender shares thoughts about the menu such as their favorite meal, popular drink or other tidbits, you ordering a second drink can almost be guaranteed!

BE AWARE OF YOUR SURROUNDINGS.

Knowing what to say and when to say it can make the difference between an affirmative yes and a resounding NO! Figuring out someone's likes and dislikes very quickly can help assess the environment and what your options may be. If the consumption of a drink is quickly coming to an end, timing your interruption of a customer's conversation is just as important as leaving a customer alone for too long and having them possibly feel ignored.

How can we adapt some of the same skills and tools into our daily lives? First, it's important to remember the little things. Remembering small details about a person's life or a coworker's story can go a long way in helping to develop trust and growth in the relationship. Also, keep in mind that a smile goes a long way! We all are busy, but the simple, non-verbal acknowledgment can send a message to the person you're interacting with that you care and you are present in the moment. Being an excellent "masterbaiter" is not necessarily a negative thing. Several positive outcomes can be derived from focusing on who you're speaking to and convincing them on your desire to care and be present. Remember, effective masterbaiting takes lots and lots of practice. Keep at it! =)

REMEMBER, THE WORST THEY CAN SAY IS NO.
THAT GIVES YOU A 50/50 CHANCE OF YES!!

SEDUCTION

WHAT CHA NEED
½ oz. Irish whiskey
1oz. vodka
3 oz. pineapple juice
½ tsp. grenadine
Pineapple wedge

WHAT CHA DO
To a cocktail shaker filled with ice,
add whiskey, vodka, pineapple juice
and grenadine.
Shake and strain into a tall glass filled with
ice. Garnish with pineapple wedge

6 KNOW WHEN TO CUT PEOPLE OFF

The best way to hang up on someone is to do it in the middle of YOUR OWN sentence! That way, they never suspect you hung up on them.

—Scorpio 6:22

As things mature, they grow and evolve. What was once appealing and enjoyable can have the tendency to become annoying and mundane. While at times it can seem insensitive to cut someone out of your life, it's actually the right thing to do. Ask Oprah! In fact, most people find it extremely necessary for personal maintenance and growth.

Let's discuss how to recognize when it's time to cut someone off, navigate difficult conversations and how to go about the sometimes physical process of removing these unwanted characters from a bar or from your life!

Before we begin, let's take an easy quiz to make sure we know the difference between an annoying person and a harmful person as it relates to your surroundings. Take out your pens, kids!

QUIZ
A - ANNOYING – H - HARMFUL

__ A friend you always have to save or rescue from a situation.

__ A friend who is always trying to get to the club while it's still free.

__ The ex lover that now does ALLL the shit you wanted to do when you were dating...with somebody else

__ The ex lover that can still get you to argue about shit from five years ago.

__ The coworker that has no idea what personal space is.

__ The coworker that constantly makes you second-guess yourself so much that you start to do the same thing to others.

__ The spouse who spends too much money but continues to get additional credit cards to fuel these spending habits.

__ The spouse who is always keeps the house at a balmy 78 degrees

So how did you do? Any friend that is in constant need of being rescued from situations and consistently looks to YOU to do that can create a toxic environment for you. Any past relationship that can still activate certain emotional triggers which should now be reserved for either yourself or your new relationship, shows signs of toxicity. If someone in the workplace is causing you to feel as if you can't make rational decisions, micromanages you and affects your daily workflow...while that is very annoying...it is also a situation that should be cut from your life. Finally, although 78 degrees is hot, it's not as sticky as forcing you into debt.

Bartenders deserve a lot more credit than what they sometimes receive. Listening to people's problems, placing orders to the kitchen, smiling at strangers, creating delicious cocktails and sometimes, unfortunately, having to make the decision on whether or not a person should have another drink is difficult. It's even more difficult when they need to make the decision to have someone removed from the establishment.

There is a general necessary responsibility a bartender has to not over serve a patron. It could not only endanger that person, but it could also put others in their path in harm's way. Additionally, it can have negative consequences for the bartender and the business. Most bartenders agree that the two main keys to successfully cut someone off is 1) the time you decide to do it and 2) the method you choose to execute the removal.

There are a few simple signs to let you know when it's time to let someone go or to cut them off (In life or at a bar).

WHEN THINGS STOP BEING FUN AND IT'S NO LONGER A MUTUALLY BENEFICIAL RELATIONSHIP.

In a bar it's quite simple. You are given the drink you ordered and in turn, you agree to pay the designated cost for the product and service. It's also expected is that you demonstrate you can handle yourself appropriately. In personal relationships, this is even more visible. When it seems one side is taking way more than they are giving, the effort begins to tilt to one side versus being an equally distributed weight.

THE PERSON'S MERE PRESENCE IS ANNOYING.

Bartenders tend to look for a combination of physical and verbal characteristics as evidence of a person's potential level of inebriation. If a customer's presence at a bar begins to disrupt other people so much that you no longer enjoy serving them, you have to take the initiative to change the atmosphere for the better. The same goes in your personal life. Avoiding calls and making up excuses to miss events means there's a good chance it's time to have a conversation with that person or simply cut ties.

THE PERSON CAN NO LONGER BE HELD ACCOUNTABLE TO BE RESPONSIBLE.

In any service relationship, there is the expectation that at the conclusion of service, the bill will be paid as well as an appropriate tip. Once this trust is compromised, it is difficult for things to go back to normal. When this factor is broken or betrayed, it can not only become irreparable, but also lead to conversations to exit the situation.

I'm sure we've all seen a drunk person at the bar. They're loud, slurring his/her words, sometimes not even remembering how many drinks they had. And it not only affects your service, it affects the bartender's ability to keep up the pace with what is expected.

So once this ultra-tipsy person has been identified, the bartender needs to go about removing them from the establishment. First thing to remember is, they ARE drunk and not able to see reality. As a bartender, you have to understand that this may take some time to accomplish. Asking some-one to leave is never easy. Most times they are unable to understand boundaries and will likely try to antagonize or intimidate the bartender. It's important to keep in mind that this may be a gradual process.

You have to remember that you are the boss of your own life or, in this instance, a bartender is the manager of the bar. You don't owe an in-depth explanation. You simply and calmly tell them how you feel, what you perceived and that you don't want them in your life or in your bar anymore. It's also not a time to argue, but simply repeat your requests or demands. It can be tricky to fall into a back-and-forth with a person and that's exactly what they want you to do.

Remember, this is not up for discussion or com-promise, so it's best to be direct, yet respectful in these situations. Also, keep in mind that there may be subsequent interactions where you will see this person again. Once a patron is asked to leave a bar, seldom are they banned. In the occasion that they return, the hope is that both parties will be able to have a cordial inter-action and not repeat any negative moments from the past. The same can happen when you cut someone out of your life. It's a small world and the chances of running into each other again are high. So be sure you can maintain a mutual respect.....but keep it moving!

Now, it doesn't mean they become your best friends again, but simply being cordial and keeping convos short and to the point should eliminate the odds of that uncomfortable situation happening.

MAKE THE CHOICE!
YOU MUST PROTECT YOURSELF
IN THE PROCESS!!

I 'MINT' WHAT I 'MINT'

WHAT CHA NEED

2-inch slice of peeled cucumber, quartered

10 mint leaves

light agave nectar

1 lime, juiced

1 ½ oz. gin, preferably Hendrick's

WHAT CHA DO

In a cocktail shaker, muddle the cucumber,
mint and agave nectar until the cucumber offers
no more resistance.

Fill a shaker with ice, then pour in the lime juice and
gin. Put the lid on your shaker and shake until the
cocktail is thoroughly chilled, about 20 seconds.

Strain the mixture into a martini glass.

Garnish with a tiny sprig of mint, if you'd like.

7
WELL vs. PREMIUM

Have you ever been to a happy hour? If you are any friend or acquaintance of mine and you are reading this book...of course you have! Most happy hours consist of discounted prices for alcoholic beverages and a few appetizers during a limited time. Generally, this happens near the end of a traditional work day when people are ready to run out of their respective 9-5's and unwind! House wines for $5, frozen margaritas for $6, well drinks for $7. People flock to these deals and try to maximize their intake for the cheapest buzz available.

The idea of drinking before dinner has its roots in the Prohibition era. When the 18th Amendment and the Volstead Act was passed banning alcohol consumption, people would host "cocktail hours", also known as "happy hours", at a speakeasy before eating at restaurants where alcohol could not be served. Cocktail lounges continued the trend of drinking before dinner. In present times, bars and lounges have happy hour before dinner as well as a special towards the end of the night. A large majority of these establishments offer discounted prices on well liquors. A well liquor is usually the cheaper liquor available at the bar.

The term comes from the "well" which is the place where bartenders have the ice, juice and the most used liquors and liqueurs. This is why you normally never see these bottles. The well liquors are kept right in front of the bartender for easy access. Most times, well liquors have less of an aging process that can affect the taste, quality and outcome of your drinking experience.

Nod your head if you've ever had a headache, nausea or simply a bad experience from these 'well' or happy hour drinks (I'm not looking). Hell, even I've done it! But sometimes, it's not worth the 'well' if you end up getting 'sick' (Get it, well.... sick? Mind blown!) Premium liquor, on the other hand, is known for having a higher quality. It's also known as Top Shelf because that is typically where it's located… on the top or premiere shelf of a bar. In terms of taste, the higher the quality of liquor used, the smoother and better it will taste for the customer.

There are several reasons premium liquor is more expensive. These companies often use all natural ingredients in their products and employ more stringent distilling practices and a longer aging process to ensure a higher quality without the use of preservatives or added sugar. However, I must make the point that price is not always indicative of purity or quality.

The concept of well and premium extends well past just barspeak. I've often thought about the 'inventory' in my personal friendship bar. I have a lot of friends that represent 'Happy Hour' for me. Our interactions are similar to a well drink. Our moments together are fast and well attended…laughs galore and they won't put a strain on my pocketbook. But many times the headaches are not worth it … the morning after regrets, the nausea when all I wanted to do was enjoy a few easy and affordable moments. That is not to say the 'well friends' have no place in our lives(I love mine), but it has to be the right time and the right place.

Who are the Well and Top Shelf friends in your life? Start paying attention to those who provide a higher quality and have fewer preservatives. Sure, you may 'pay' more as it relates to effort or investment, but when in doubt, always think about this: when you notice a person at a bar that is very particular of what they are putting into their body, don't you view them a little different..almost in an admirable way? It's as if each drink is purposeful and the selection intentional. I don't know about you, but I can ALWAYS taste the difference when I choose to upgrade.

Remember, deciding not to choose is still making a choice. Proverbs 27: 19-21 says that a mirror reflects a man's face, but what he is really like is shown by the friends he chooses.(FYI, that's from the Bible=))We all should have well and premium in our life, just be sure to monitor why, what and when you are consuming and if you can afford the after effects!

WHO WILL YOU CHOOSE TO CONSUME NEXT TIME?

QUALI-TEA

WHAT CHA NEED
(TOP SHELF OR WELL)
1/2 oz. orange liqueur
1/2 oz. rum, 1/2 oz. gin
1/2 oz. vodka, 1/2 oz. tequila
1 oz. sour mix, 2 oz. Cola (or enough
to fill the glass)
Garnish: lemon wedge

WHAT CHA DO
Add all ingredients together.
Shake with ice and pour into a tall glass.

BE CAREFUL STARTING A BAR TAB

I vividly remember the first time I ever fell in love. I met her in college during my freshman year. I was struggling to make ends meet and she said she could help me out financially. Now, I'm no strumpet or lady of the night but I was down to hear her out. We discussed the terms of our 'arrangement', what was expected of me and the boundaries of our limitations. At the end of the day, with her assistance, I was able to pay for a majority of my expenses and enjoy college stress-free. We actually ended up having so much fun together! Trips, fine dining, gifts, it was great!! It wasn't until my senior year that things started to go south. I was just about to graduate and start my first official corporate job. It started to feel that we were outgrowing each other.... but she didn't see it that way.

I wanted a clean break and a chance to live my life independent of her, but she started calling saying she wanted me back.... Sending me letters, calling my family members and friends. It was very stalker like! I will admit I cared for her, but to me she served her purpose. Odd thing is, to this day, she still hits me up from time to time even though she has since moved on to many other relationships. I'm still working on getting rid of her, but honestly, she's hard to forget. I guess you never forget your first love and I will never forget mine. Her initials are S.M. aka Sallie Mae.

Hopefully, you now know that I'm talking about Sallie Mae, the student loan service now called Navient.

The truth is, whether or not you have student loans or credit card debt, we can all probably relate to running up an amount we owe. Sometimes the debt we incur is not even of the monetary kind. Over the years I've seen many coworkers not manage their time wisely. Adding project upon project, committing to serve on boards and volunteer for multiple community outreach efforts only to be met with the reality that they've taken on too much and don't have the mental bandwidth to complete everything. This is even the same with personal relationships. If you are running up tabs of affection and honesty, make sure you have the love and affection to give as payment. Also, overcommitting to too many people can leave you scrambling for extra time as currency. Starting an open tab or tally of any kind has its dangers. Without periodically checking in to see the balance, one can find themselves overdrawn on time and money.

Bartenders see this all too often. One minute you rush to make it to happy hour for those five dollar drinks and two dollar tacos, and a few hours later with one creative and friendly bartender, at the end of the night you're looking at a tab of over $200. We used to call this **DWD- Drinking while Debting**.

So before starting a bar tab of any kind, make sure you can afford what you're going to spend and be able to fully pay the bill at the end of the evening. Always make sure you have the currency accepted to pay that debt.

Not to be forgotten, there is also a danger in splitting tabs. At the end of the jovial moment, many people forget what they ordered and have a difficult time owning up and settling their debt. There always seems to be an issue when things just don't add up at the end of the bill. Some people forget the tiny add-ons like an extra side of fries or adding chicken on a Caesar salad. I would be lying if I said I never saw arguments, cancelled Ubers, fights and even friendships end because there is still a large amount of a bill outstanding and everyone suddenly gets a case of amnesia. I even recall a situation when an overly inebriated guest, who was part of a large party, caused a ruckus demanding that whoever ordered 'Gratuity' pony up his or her share...smh

It's a cautionary tale. Whenever you have an 'open tab' in your life, make sure you check on the running total frequently. When it's time to pay up most people and places don't take an I.O.U.!

CONSTANTLY CHECK ON
THE ACCUMULATION OF ANY DEBT!

ACT YOUR WAGE

WHAT CHA NEED
2 oz. gin
1/4 oz. extra dry vermouth
1/4 oz. olive juice
green olives

WHAT CHA DO
Combine the gin, vermouth, and olive juice
in a cocktail shaker and stir.
Strain into a chilled martini glass.
Garnish with as many olives as you'd like
on a toothpick.

LGBT
(LET'S GET BETTER AT TIPPING)

How well do you tip? Be Honest! When you are at a restaurant or a bar and you've received great service, do you reflect that in additional dollars? Do you feel the service should happen automatically and you should not compensate additionally for it? Many think the answer to that question depends on if you have ever truly worked in the service industry. If you read the pre-drinks section of this book, (if you didn't, please go back now;)) you will remember one of my first jobs in college was being a server. I definitely believe in paying it forward and as it relates to tipping, it has come in handy when special requests are made or when a bar is extremely busy. My friends can attest to the fact that when we walk into our favorite bar, most times my drink is already being poured before we even find a seat. This is not only because I am known as a regular but also because I have always tipped appropriately.

So where did tipping actually originate? A little backstory...the origin of the word tip can present quite the conspiracy theory. Many historians say tips started as a way to pay bare minimum to freed slaves while getting cheap labor for businesses(I do believe this to be true) But depending on who you ask, this word could have popped up in the 13th or 20th century. For the purposes of this book, I would like to use the definitions of tip as it appears through an acronym which can mean three different things:

- To Ensure Promptness
- To Ensure Performance
- To Ensure Prompt Service

If these acronyms were true, then it would actually be spelled **T.E.P** versus **T.I.P.**, since the word 'ensure' would be the correct word to use in this case. Some suggest for a tip to be truly successful, it should be given PRIOR to service, much like in the olden days when cowboys paid someone a shiny gold coin to watch their horse outside the saloon 'before' going in.

Some people believe that if you award the tip prior to service, it can further guarantee attention to detail and a pleasant experience.

Depending on where you live in the country, the standard tip can range anywhere from 15% to 20%. Many Americans have problems giving additional money outside of the initial service provided, but a tip is a great way to offer added incentive, encouragement and positive reinforcement.

How do you 'ensure' a quality performance or experience in your daily life? Speaking every day to the doorman or assistant at work is not only gracious and appropriate, but could also benefit you should you need assistance with something in the future. Showing up to a friend's event when you KNOW all you really want to do is go home, stay in bed and watch TV, cannot only help grow that friendship, but this can be a person who is there for you when the tables are turned.

A few years ago in New York I was taking an express train into work. There was a young woman who started sweating and leaning over as if she was going to vomit or pass out. An elderly woman who was a few seats down from her, reached into her bag and gave a small clementine and a tissue to the obviously ill passenger. The girl took a few bites of the fruit, wiped her brow and actually started to feel better. Although they did not know each other, this woman made an additional investment in a stranger. I'm sure one day this will be reciprocated.

I witnessed this type of kindness again a few years later. On a crowded city bus I saw a group of people TIP a total stranger. As the packed bus pulled up to its next stop, an asshole in a suit barreled his way towards the exit near the front of the bus. On his obnoxiously awkward way out, he knocked a phone out of the hands of an unsuspecting teen wearing a uniform from a fast food restaurant. On further inspection, not only was the cell phone screen cracked, the teen had a bag in his other hand that indicated he had just purchased the phone. Devastated, the teen just lowered his head... likely contemplating next steps. And that's when it happened. First one, then two...finally several passengers on the bus who witnessed the accident, started passing money to the teen. Some gave quarters and others donated several dollars. Knowing how expensive phones are, and sensing his disappointment, random strangers stepped in to help.

You don't have to be a bartender or server to know what it feels like to be tipped. Paying it forward goes far beyond a bar. Be it a smile, a kind word, an orange or a dollar, you can help make someone's day or life better.

Get to tipping!!

ALWAYS PAY IT FORWARD!

PRIDE & PREJUDICE

WHAT CHA NEED
3 oz. Prosecco
2 oz. Aperol
1 oz. Soda water

WHAT CHA DO
Add all ingredients into a wine glass
with ice and stir.
Garnish with an orange wheel.

WHO HAS YOUR BACK?

I've had the privilege of living in Harlem, at Mile Marker 22 of the New York City Marathon for over 8 years. On the first Sunday in November, for almost 10 hours, I can see every single runner pass my window to a bevy of cheers, cowbells, whistles and support for the sacrifice and training they have done to complete this amazing accomplishment. Even when the sun sets and the last two or three runners are willing themselves to the finish line, supporters are still out there helping to push them to keep going. It's truly beautiful. With all of the preparation and physical ability it takes to run this world famous marathon, each runner or cyclist needs a support system. A group they have assembled to get them through the challenging times and to encourage them when their mental or physical struggles arise.

Life can also be compared to a marathon. We need people in our corner to help cheer us on through the highs and lows. And although we are actively in the race and the focus is generally on the main participant/runner, what many fail to see is the important role those behind the scenes play. Most times, when we sit at a bar, we notice the people around us, the inventory behind the bar, and the bartender. The person most of us least remembers, is the barback. When the bar is crowded and someone behind the bar approaches, we tend to get excited and think a bartender is available. Then the person tells you they can only give you water or ice. Doh! Nine times out of ten, this is the bar back. At first glance the barback position can seem like a menial role. In actuality, barbacks are an essential component to a bartending staff's success. A key objective to a barback is to always offer assistance to other team members who are preparing drinks.

So what does a barback really do? They get the bar ready for service. That can mean cutting garnishes, folding napkins, filling the straw and coaster holders, etc. You can normally spot this person because they are constantly moving and seldom touch the cash register or speak with guests.

Being a barback definitely has its challenges. There's not a lot of appreciation for barbacking, yet it can be an extremely physically demanding job. Running around all night refilling ice buckets and carrying crates full of dirty and washed drinkware is enough to burn a day's worth of calories! A successful barback constantly has his or her eyes and ears open so they can anticipate the needs of the bartender. Restocking the alcohol, mixers and garnishes before they run out really helps keep the business flowing.

As I stated before, the main role of a barback is to be an essential support mechanism to a bartender, the bartending team or the restaurant.

Who are the main supporting characters in your life? A good friend is always there to have your back. They pay attention to when you are running low on love, energy or motivation. A true friend can anticipate what you need before it happens and restock you with positive energy or words of affirmation. When things get busy in your life, this person has your back and is able to keep things on track 24-7.

I do not want to present the barback role as a down and dirty job where no one appreciates them or they are undervalued. On the contrary, think about a time have you ever been to a bar without barback assistance? To witness even the most seasoned bartender scramble for clean glassware and restocking their own supplies can be very unappealing and make the bartender and restaurant look unprofessional. I would even go so far as to say that I don't believe a bartender can be fully successful without a strong person by their side to assist them.

So the next time you go to a bar, pay attention to who is keeping that ship afloat and making your experience run as smooth as possible. And when you get that text, email, hug or face-to-face word of encouragement from your friends, remember who was helping keep you motivated to serve all the people in your life. Offer them a word of thanks...

HAVING SOMEONE'S BACK........

CAN SAVE A LIFE!!!

I GOT CHU

WHAT CHA NEED

2 oz. Hennessy V.S or V.S.O.P Privilege
.75 oz. Grand Marnier
.5 oz. Fresh Lemon Juice
Garnish: Lemon Twist and sugared rim
Glass: Coupe or Martini

WHAT CHA DO

Add all ingredients to a shaker with ice,
shake until chilled, strain into a chilled
cocktail or martini glass, garnish with a
lemon twist, and an optional sugared rim.

11 PEST CONTROL

Encountering an annoyance or two in our lives is common. From robocalls to excessive crowds, we each have our top two or three pet peeves that can send us over the flippin' top! Bartenders deal with similar distractions. And I'm not talking about customers. Nothing says lack of care or unprofessionalism than a dirty bar, dirty house or dirty office.

Fruit flies and gnats are not only annoying as hell, they give the impression of a dirty bar and can end up being bad for business. But even the most diligent cleaning and containment of fruit will not stop these pesky, winged visitors from finding a way into an establishment.

Here's what I know about the characteristics of fruit flies and gnats:

- Both seem to pop up out of nowhere
- They are annoying as hell so rapid removal is essential
- Sweet things or decaying organic matter are the main attractants

Containing or eliminating flies and gnats is crucial for a healthy service environment and proper management of any establishment. The best strategy for dealing with them requires you to be swift and proactive. The two choices you have are: Fight or Flight! You can impose a strategy to eliminate the infestation and prevent further breeding, or you can simply exit the premises or area where this pesky annoyance occurs. First thing to do is to start at the source.

ASSESS AND DISPOSE OF YOUR TRASH REGULARLY

Sounds easy enough right? If you have ever forgotten to take out the trash from the night before you notice that awful smell can spread throughout the place. If this is not immediately taken care of, what's next is the unwelcome sight of winged and unfriendly visitors. Open trash sitting around gives the things that are attracted to it an environment in which to thrive. Just as humans need food, water and shelter, flies and gnats need decaying food, fruit and unclean areas to set up shop and lay their eggs.

Many of us take a yearly inventory of our social media pages, deleting people from Facebook or Instagram who seem to 'lay their eggs or seeds of doubt in our lives. For some reason they were attracted to you, but once you realize their purpose is annoying rather than beneficial to your spirit, you need to dispose of the things that keep them there.

BE CAREFUL OF CONTAMINATION

Flies and gnats spread germs whenever they come in contact with a source. This is why it's always important for bartenders to seal or cover alcohol and mixers at the end of a shift. You may have noticed towards the end of the night a bartender using pour spout caps, saran wrap or small cups to cover liquid. This is because left unattended, some of the valuable ingredients can be contaminated by these pesky visitors.

When people in your life are buzzing around with no intention but to spread infection and negative things, the potential of further damage depends on when and how you choose to solve the issue. But remember, sometimes it's not what we are attracted to, but what we attract. Of the annoyances in your life, have you ever stopped to think which ones you are responsible for? Are you providing an energy that is actually attracting the very thing that is driving you up the wall? Take care of what you value. Once its contaminated, it may no longer be of use to you. Bottle up and protect yourself from potential gnats and flies!

ALWAYS PROTECT WHAT YOU VALUE!
PESTS WILL ALWAYS TRY TO INVADE.

STRANGE FRUIT

WHAT CHA NEED

3 oz. Red Wine

3/4 oz. Cognac

1/2 oz. Orange Juice

1/2 oz. Lime Juice

1/2 oz. Lemon Juice

Lemon Lime Soda

Strawberries & Blueberries

WHAT CHA DO

Drop fruits into base of wine glass and pour over
lemon juice, lime juice and orange juice.
Add red wine and cognac and stir lightly.
Top with lemon lime soda.

12 WORKING THROUGH A BAD DAY

You could shit rainbows, sneeze glitter and have puppy wallpaper in your home...but no matter how nice you are, you have most certainly had a bad day. When it comes to the workplace, many times our worlds collide and we are unable to hide away the issues and worries in our personal life. We've all had those days when it feels like nothing is happening the way it should. Many people are able to simply shut their doors or slot in a fake meeting or two to give them a tiny reprieve from the daily grind. For those in the service/hospitality industry, this is not so simple. A majority of time is spent interacting with customers or fellow employees, answering questions and being constantly on the go while dealing with rude people, doing inventory or spending hours on your feet.

The key to surviving is to try to leave work issues at work and home issues at home. I know this is easier said than done.

In 2010, a flight attendant on a delayed plane screamed at passengers and proceeded to dare them to leave the plane if they had "the balls" to do it. He continued to yell over the intercom, "If anyone has the balls to want to get off, I'll let you get off! Get off! I'm not responsible for the weather. I don't care anymore. This is probably my last flight," several witnesses quoted him saying. Clearly, this person had some pre-existing emotional struggles.

That same year, another flight attendant appeared to snap. Prior to takeoff and after a dispute with a passenger, a seasoned flight attendant grabbed the phone from the PA system and let loose a colorful monologue. Authorities said he grabbed a beer from the beverage cart, pulled the lever that activated the emergency-evacuation chute and slid down, making a daring exit.

Now, if I were on that plane I would be sipping my Jack, recording on my phone and watching the fireworks. However, years later, I thought about what it truly takes to be a flight attendant. Safety precautions, serving, cleaning (food and some-times feces), dealing with unruly passengers, crying babies and turbulence. As challenging as this is, imagine also having marital issues at home, financial difficulties or even health/mental complications. It is truly a lot to deal with.

The bartender's role is no different. In addition to needing a strong knowledge of drinks, being a cashier, server, friend, bouncer and therapist... to be successful at bartending, personality and charm must be turned on at all times to make the difference between a first and a fourth drink order...between a one-time visitor and a repeat customer. No matter how horrible your day may be, every customer experience needs to be indi-vidual and meaningful. Next time you find your-self at work while life is active on your mind, try to self regulate and focus on the present...before unemployment becomes another worry!

TRY TO STAY PRESENT IN THE MOMENT!!

WERK HORSE

WHAT CHA NEED

4 oz. ginger beer
2 oz. vodka
Juice of half a lime
Lime slice, for garnish

WHAT CHA DO

Add ginger beer, vodka, and lime to
a Moscow Mule mug or a highball
glass filled with ice. Stir.
Garnish with a lime slice.

13 MIX WELL WITH OTHERS

Now, you don't have to be a seasoned bartender to know there are certain things you should never mix with alcohol:

Medication
Red Bull
Driving
Texting an Ex
Low Account Balances
Amazon shopping
Abstinence
Watching those damn ASPCA infomercials that ask you for money!

Even in everyday life, certain combinations and mixtures can be volatile. Wouldn't it be amazing if we could choose the people we get to mix or interact with in life? What if you literally had the ability to select each person you work with at your job? Or you got to choose the people who sit next to you on a bus, subway or bar. I'm convinced that a majority of us would live a nice life, full of relaxation and joy! However, we all know life doesn't work like that and the likelihood of being with 100% of the personalities that you get along with are slim to none. Even if you are lucky enough to work with someone you get along with, who's to say that the shit will last?

There are tons of examples of people who have been together both romantically and professionally but while the romance fizzled, the work contract is ironclad. The show must go on! Take for example, power couple Domenico Dolce and Stefano Gabbana. These fashion icons worked together for over three decades. Yet even after their very public breakup, they were still able to make that coint...... Yes, I said coin with a T! But what if you are not as strong as this successful duo? If you are unable to choose who you work with, there may always be clear differences in your approach to business and ways of communicating.

The key is this....it doesn't matter! We have to learn how to play or 'mix' well with others. You can't mix oil and water, but there may sometimes be a situation where they have to exist together in the same container or environment. In the service industry, one never knows who the hell is going to walk through that door. Regardless of who it is, the server has the duty and responsibility to be cordial and provide service with a smile. =)

A bartender can encounter hundreds of different people and personalities in a given night. Clearly, a love connection with all of them is highly unlikely, but nonetheless, they must be given the same level of respect and service. After taking a poll with several current and former bartenders, here are the top five types of personalities they have encountered at a bar. Go make your favorite cocktail and let's discuss the top 5 personalities encountered at the bar:

TOP FIVE BAR PATRON PERSONALITIES:
(IN NO PARTICULAR ORDER.)

Note: If you are one of these people …Well, just keep reading)

Inebriated Einstein - You've met 'em…they know it all and no one can tell them any different…from gentrification statistics in New York City to what's in Capone's vault to what 'really' happened to Whitney Houston. This visitor gets more 'intelligent' as the drinks and the night continue. It is impossible to rationalize with this eager beaver…after all, they can't help that you have no idea what they are talking about. Most bar Einstein's have some area of their lives that's not quite where they want it to be. Seeking validation, these fluttering factual phenoms keep the immediate crowd entertained with pop culture, historical and anecdotal tidbits. Next time you encounter one, let them know how smart they are. ;)

Rowdy Ryan - Ever notice how some people get louder the more they drink? I guess that's why they say alcohol content is listed by "volume"! Introducing Rowdy Ryan! This character usually walks in a bar unassuming and quiet and places a drink order like the average customer. A couple of drinks in and slowly their volume begins to increase as well as the amount of irritated people. Overreacting to a moderately funny joke, yelling across the bar to an old friend (or stranger) and annoying surrounding clients, Rowdy Ryan can be one of the worst patrons at a bar. This character would normally go unnoticed at a loud tavern or sports bar, but nooooo, they always seem to be at the chiller, calmer spots. Rowdy Ryan, we hear you...unfortunately!!

Happy Hour Helen - If an establishment is having happy hour from 5-7pm, this person is there from 4:59-7:01pm. Helen totally maximizes discounts and seldom strays off that menu. Once it is announced that Happy Hour is over, the tab is closed and they are out the door! I have no issue with Helen. She has a good time, knows her budget and keeps it moving!

Insatiable Iris - I mean, why did you come out in the first place?!? This patron refuses to believe anything is ever right. This hard to please customer is never satisfied and keeps the attention of the bartender with complaints like, my drink's too weak, too strong, food is too salty, etc. It's pretty difficult to produce a pleasant experience for this customer. The best you can do is hope they run out of things to complain about. Generally, Iris is not satisfied with one or more aspects of her personal life and in order to make it better, she controls what she can...her level of service.

Chatty Charles - This person likely lives alone, comes to the bar alone and will talk to ANYONE who will listen. There is absolutely no awareness that the person next to them may be preoccupied with a date, on the phone, eating or even placing an order. Charles will WAIT until they are done to make sure full attention can be offered. After poking around to see your relationship status, you might be propositioned for a date or the next 'unplanned' meetup. All in all, Charles is just lonely and in need of interaction.

Not to be outdone, there are a comparable Top Five Personalities in the workplace, too! How well do you mix with them?

TOP FIVE WORK PERSONALITIES:
(IN NO PARTICULAR ORDER.)

Kiss up Keith - Oh…no, that's not Nutella on his lips! Keith will find a way to be at the right place at the right time for the right kiss up opportunity. And to add insult to injury, Keith moonlights as a professional 'under the bus' thrower. This coworker's modus operandi is to take out the weak to make him look strong!

Micromanager Marcus - If you haven't worked for this type you definitely know someone who has. It's a challenging task to work for a personality that breaks down and oversees every… little…instruction…or…task. It's very frustrating! Most micromanagers have issues with trust. They want the job done right and instead of using the opportunity as a teachable or training moment, they are more concerned with getting the job done correctly because their name is attached to it.

Over Delegating Oscar - The original ask was simple: make a list of all team members interested in volunteering for a company-wide initiative. Oscar will ask you to set up a meeting to discuss the main meeting strategy for the approach to the meeting to ask for volunteers. Then Oscar will have you assemble an exploratory team to craft an email to send back for approval. You would tell him to fuck himself, but alas...he likely would just have you do that too! Oscar has misinterpreted what leadership really means vs. excessive oversight.

Inappropriate Eliza - Hmmm, no I did not know your mom's uterine fibroids were the size of a cantaloupe or that you have always dreamt about sleeping with the boss...AND me! This one is self-explanatory. Eliza is in desperate need of connecting, but is throwing oversharing Hail Mary's to do so. No consideration of crossing the line. Eliza is determined to connect...by any means necessary.

Gimme Greg - Greg started at your company FIVE days ago. Already he is inquiring..."What's the timeline for promotion? Can I work from home three days a week? Can we set up a time to discuss a salary increase and cost of living adjustment?" To the naked eye, Greg is just a hungry go get-ter...with his eyes on the prize because he knows a closed mouth won't get fed. WRONG!!! Greg has been cursed with a sense of entitlement. With no true examples of putting in the work, he will likely always miss an opportunity due to looking around for the next thing.

So be it at a bar or in the office, you will likely meet many unsavory characters that, although you may not like, you will have to work with. No need to be shaken, muddled and bitter about it (get it?). A bartender's success lies in realizing it's not about befriending every customer, instead, it's about extending the same respect to every customer regardless of position or personality. Next time you encounter a 'spirit' that may be challenging, work on a personality cocktail to make the situation taste better.

PLAY NICE IN THE SANDBOX OF LIFE!

BEE NICE

WHAT CHA NEED
2 oz. bourbon
3/4 oz. freshly squeezed juice
from 1 lemon
3/4 oz. honey syrup

WHAT CHA DO
Combine all ingredients in an ice-filled shaker.
Shake until well chilled, about 10 seconds.
Strain into an ice-filled glass.

LIQUID COURAGE

"Trust me, you CAN dance."

—Whiskey

As a kid, I never wanted to disappoint my grandparents. After all, they continued to take care of me and raise me after my mom died. I worked hard in school, brought home straight A's and ended up getting enough scholarship awards to pay for my undergraduate and graduate degrees. However, shortly after I started college it became hard for me to focus on my graciously paid for studies.

I never liked lying and it became evident I needed to share something I had known for years with my grandparents, who were two of the most important people in my life. I wanted to talk about my inner self rather than my sexuality. Essentially, I needed to come out to my grandparents. The goal was to tell them separately so I could address each of their questions independently. First up was my grandfather, JD. He was actually most necessary because I had started to notice him gently flirting with my girlfriend, lol. That fateful day I pulled up to the house, went into the kitchen and made a double vodka and cranberry. After I downed the drink, I reviewed my notes, I walked to his bedroom and asked to speak to him. Showing the strength he had instilled in me as a child, and the courage the alcohol had provided, I shared the truth I had known since I was very young. When I finished speaking and crying, JD looked at me, smiled, sat up in bed and said…"I'm about to go to the store, do you want anything?" Perplexed and frustrated I yelled, "Did you hear what I said?!!" He stood up and grabbed his hat and wallet and then said, "I've always known, pumpkin." Then he walked out the door. Well shit, had I been the only one walking around thinking I was fooling someone?

LOL! I bet those damn Hilliary Clinton kitten heels gave me away.

With this new bit of knowledge I was a bit more relaxed to tell Nunna, my grandmother. Nonetheless, I found myself making another drink to calm my nerves.

This time I went with a trusty shot of Jameson. I walked in to repeat the speech and surprisingly, although she seemed initially shocked, she was extremely supportive! She told me she loved me and nothing would change that. For the weeks and months that followed, things continued to be great between me and my grandparents! Unfortunately, later that year, my grandmother's health started to decline. Shortly after, she was diagnosed with Alzheimer's, which is a very confusing and fast acting disease. It strips you of your memory as you forget key facts that can inhibit future interactions with friends and family. Soooooooo, yeah......the next year I came out to my grandmother AGAIN...twice when I was 22 years old. Damn, when I was 32.....that was a tough time. :)

But amazingly, each time I had to retell the story, she was totally supportive and understanding. Although I ended up having this conversation multiple times, I got stronger each time I did, and so did our bond!

If you have ever cried at a bar for whatever reason, told someone off or gotten something off your chest, you know the therapeutic relief that can come from letting go of holding in difficult feelings, giving in to the weight of emotions and allowing yourself to exist in your truth. I used to wonder why some people would get extra emotional after having a few drinks...it's because they feel that at that particular time, they CAN! The typical concern of others watching or caring about others opinions is the least of their worries.

Liquid Courage...there is just something about the overpowering effects of liquid courage that can allow people to be their real selves. But is this a true statement?

While you can find supporting articles and documentation that supports alcohol as a tool to lower inhibitions and make one more prone to speaking their truth…it's not a method I generally support. Several people use alcohol as a catalyst for confronting the uncomfortable, and as an ignitor for needed bravery. But as most know, there is definitely a danger to using alcohol to achieve these results.

Instead of alcohol, courage is a better tool to use during difficult conversations or interactions. Courage is the ability to step out on faith without the support of a safety net that could provide a false sense of security. Courage is the understanding that regardless of the outcome, you face something head on…even if you are unclear of the consequence. And while the drinks I had before a difficult conversation may have led me to believe I was in a calmer, stronger state, it probably wasn't true.

As a bartender, the first liquid courage bar fight I encountered was a scary one. Everything seemed fine that night until these two guys, (who had been drinking for some time) got into an argument about which football team is better, the New York

Giants or the New Orleans Saints. The argument escalated into a shoving match, punches being thrown and ultimately both being kicked out of the bar. It was such an unnecessary altercation. I mean honestly, we all know the Dallas Cowboys are America's Team :) But I knew the only reason the fight took place was because 'liquid courage' made one aggressor feel like he could open a can of whoop ass on a stranger.

Bartenders have to keep a keen eye out for those with the Popeye Syndrome. Once someone pops a can of Spinach (or several drinks) they can quickly become belligerent and dangerous. I equate the danger to liquid courage to your mouth writing a check that your ass can't cash.

It doesn't have to be alcohol that's used as a courage booster. Going above your financial means to own a certain car, buying the latest phone you can't afford so you can appear to be with the in crowd or surgically altering your body to get others approval instead of for your own desire could be signs of using something to help your confidence in front of others.

The downside to using material things or alcohol to lower your anxiety, is that it could actually make you more dependent on it, cause additional anxiety, and truly give a false sense of reality or self esteem. If you find yourself using something to alter your courage or how you are viewed by others, make sure you use a two-way mirror. You might not look how you think!

IF YOU WANT TO BE COURAGEOUS, MAKE SURE YOUR PRESENTED SELF AND PERCEIVED SELF ARE THE SAME!

ZERO PROOF

WHAT CHA NEED

1 oz. lemon juice

1 oz. orange juice

1 oz. pineapple juice

Dash grenadine

2 oz. ginger ale (or club soda)

Optional: 2 dashes Angostura Bitters

Garnish: pineapple and orange slices

WHAT CHA DO

Pour the juices, grenadine, and bitters into a cocktail shaker filled with ice. Shake well. Strain into a chilled Collins glass filled with fresh ice. Top with ginger ale. Garnish with pineapple or orange slice.

15 THE NIGHTCAP

In the Urban dictionary (leave me alone, that IS an actual thing), one popular definition of the nightcap is that it's used as a thinly veiled euphemism for sex. In movies, when a man or woman invites.. well, a man or a woman =) up for a nightcap, that means it's usually going down! I tried using the 'come in for a nightcap' back in the day. I must have been doing it wrong because all that normally ended up going down was my self esteem and all my good tequila. However, we now know the term nightcap can also mean an alcoholic drink taken at bedtime to 'help' you sleep.

In the docu-film, *The Truth About Alcohol*, theories are investigated around the nightcap. Through A/B testing, it was discovered that having a cocktail before bed actually does NOT help you sleep better. You can fall asleep faster but the quality of sleep is diminished. Most people, myself included, love a nightcap before bed. My personal selection is a Jameson Caskmate or 12 year Redbreast on the rocks. Deep down, I know it does not help me accomplish anything extra, but it honestly, it gives me a sense of relief and a solo toast to a job or day well done.

The chapters I discussed in this book: Knowing when to cut people off, what are you serving or advertising, who has your back, well vs. premium people or items..... all simple phrases that you never thought would be interchangeable with your work, home and bar life! Now, these phrases will hopefully cross industries, conversations and cultural lines. As I said in the beginning of this book, the goal was to draw some fun and creative parallels between the bartender and the bar patron world.

Becoming a successful bartender takes effort and practice, much like becoming a great friend, partner or sibling. Bartenders are the face of whatever bar they tend, so it's important to make sure they are contributing to the ambience and energy of the establishment. A truly effective bartender is one who provides a consistent, quality product, has an excellent recall on whatever a regular's favorite cocktail is and, if called upon, can be somewhat of an expert on any topic from politics, to sex toys, to fashion and relationships. In addition to being all of these things, bartenders also have to make sure they are aware of the surroundings at all times. Watching whose drink is almost empty, keeping a close eye on bar inventory and making sure no one walks out without paying the tab are just as important as the drink being prepared.

This is the same creative and challenging multi-tasking that we do as friends, partners and coworkers. You will never be able to please or serve everyone at the same time. The goal is to focus, pace yourself and not get too overwhelmed. And every once in a while, it's ok to take some time for you… to decompress and get re-centered. When you feel down and close to depletion, Think Like a Bartender! Look at your inventory to reassess your needs. Make sure you are restocked with the essentials. Remember your regulars... those who have been with you since day one. Stay armed with charm and make sure every client in your life is given adequate service and equal treatment. Like a Bartender, play well with others! You don't have to be best friends or love someone to give them service or respect. If you find it's time to cut them off, be firm yet fair.

Beware of the need of liquid courage and remember to separate your well vs. premium items to ensure your best personal happy hour. Finally, if it's a situation you can no longer be in, it's ok to fire yourself. And regardless of whether you are having a bad day, remember who loves you and has your back! Take these recipes for life (and the cocktails) and create a better you. The next time you see a bartender, give them a nod of acknowledgement and realize you both have more in common than you think.

CHEERS!

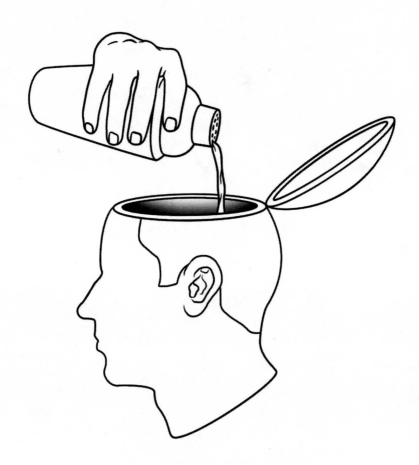

THINK LIKE A BARTENDER

IT'S ALL CONNECTED

WHAT CHA NEED
1 ½ oz. cognac
1 ½ oz. amaretto liqueur
Ice
Orange peel to garnish

WHAT CHA DO
Pour cognac and amaretto
into a glass, over ice.
Garnish with orange peel twist,
and enjoy.

ABOUT THE AUTHOR

A multi-faceted leader, L.D. Morrow has over 20 years' experience in various corporate roles from Fortune 500 companies.

She's performed stand up at New York's famous Caroline's on Broadway, Broadway Comedy Club and other notable venues. L.D's southern charm and quick wit makes her a continued sought after personality who hosts red carpets and moderates panel events around the country. L.D. is also an Associate Producer for the 2019 film Burden.

Born and raised in Houston, TX, she holds a Master of Arts in Strategic Communication and Leadership from Seton Hall University, an MBA from the Jones School of Business at Texas Southern University and is a graduate of leading industry programs, CTAM-U at Harvard Business School and the acclaimed Digital Marketing program at Cornell University. A lover of Tequila and Irish Whiskeys, L.D. can often be found cracking jokes and making cocktails for her friends and family.